To dear Paul

Merry Christmas 2009!

Lots of love

Julio & Jeff
xox

Come back soon! x.

beyond reasonable drought

beyond reasonable drought

Photographs of a Changing Land and its People

Many Australian Photographers Group

The Five Mile Press

State Library
of Victoria

The Five Mile Press Pty Ltd
1 Centre Road, Scoresby
Victoria 3179 Australia
www.fivemile.com.au

Published in association with
State Library of Victoria
328 Swanston Street, Melbourne
Victoria 3000 Australia
www.slv.vic.gov.au

First published 2009

Printed in China

Designed by Phil Campbell
Map collation pp214-15 Kristy Lund and Rodney Dekker

National Library of Australia cataloguing-in-publication entry
    Beyond reasonable drought : photographs of a changing land and its people / Many Australian Photographers Group.

    1st ed.

    978 1 74211 096 7 (hbk)

    Droughts--Australia--Pictorial works.
    Australians--Pictorial works.
    Australia--Rural conditions--Pictorial works.

    MAP Group.

    363.349290994

A number of the photographs in this book were given by the photographers to the subjects of the photos or to their communities. In addition some of the images have been acquired by various national, state and regional institutions. The photographs on pages 9, 133, 143, 154, 155, 184 and 188 are in the Pictures Collection of the State Library of Victoria.

Photographs in preliminary pages
Page ii: View from Tallangatta lookout, Lake Hume at about five per cent full. Tallangatta, Victoria, 2006, photographer Rodney Dekker

Page vi: Farmer Howard Flanner inspects the soil on his land, twenty kilometres north of Ouyen. Ouyen, Victoria, 2006, photographer Rodney Dekker

Foreword Don Watson

My local paper says that while last November was much wetter than usual, inflows into district storages were less than ten per cent of the ten-year average, and the ten-year average is half the long-term average. The volume of water reaching the reservoirs was only six per cent of the long-term average. In these 'dry inflow conditions' such rain as manages to fall is swallowed at once by the land. I do not know how they estimate such things, but the water authorities say that in the coming year there is no more than a one in ten chance that 'wet inflow conditions' will be exceeded; a five in ten chance that 'average inflow conditions' will be exceeded; and a nine in ten chance that 'dry inflow conditions' will be exceeded. As far as I can tell, this seems to mean that our long drought is not about to end.

The figures are measures of what anyone living in the drought has known for years: by living, I mean anyone at least half aware of the weather, soil and plants and the habits and colours of the seasons, and possessing some memory of active springs and watercourses, ice on puddles, and the sound of real persistent rain.

Call it impoverished to be oblivious to these things, yet it is also a blessing unknown to nearly everyone in the record of humanity. That an economy can grow and people flourish in the midst of drought; that they can measure it only by the level of the reservoirs and that 155 litres of water a day per person should be the worst it comes down to – these are freaks of history.

We who are conscious of the feebleness of modern showers, the vanished springs, the slow drying up, even if our livelihoods don't depend upon the weather, feel as if our lives do.

We are wired for drought: not quite as kangaroos are, but deep in our psyche and culture. In the Old Testament, drought is the dread affliction, the great metaphor for barrenness, failure and extinction. Always it is a punishment wrought by God and lifted only by his mercy. In the Koran it is 'God who sendeth forth the winds which raise the clouds aloft; then drives them on to some land dead from drought, and gives life thereby to the earth after its death. So shall be the Resurrection.'

So long as God has been visiting dry inflow conditions upon us, it has been to God we have prayed for deliverance. 'Send her down, Huey!' the outback plea for rain, is a laconic version of the most ancient mantra. Men and women also plead for something to 'satisfy [their] soul in drought', to be 'like a watered garden, a spring … whose waters do not fail'.

There is no denying the power of these metaphors, even when we know it is folly to go on believing that only a deity susceptible to our entreaties can return us to average inflow conditions. We could do with metaphors of equal power to ground us in ways to live with a nature no less formidable than God, but within easier reach of understanding – and what's of more consequence, vulnerable not to our prayers but to our behaviour.

If, as seems likely, this drought turns out to be not a drought but a new climate of our own making, for those alive to the effects it will still be much like every other drought since Job. It will still depress and enervate us – 'gut' us, as farmers say. It will still make unreasonable demands on hope and endurance, and make character in doing so.

In the absence of words that rise much above 'prolonged dry weather events impacting on inflow conditions', we have these photographs that, in the various unpredictable ways of the camera, capture the ancient drama now unfolding, and the hope of resurrection.

Don Watson

Introduction Andrew Chapman

In 2006, after eight years of informal participation in rural-based community photographic projects, the Many Australian Photographers Group (MAP Group) was officially formed. MAP Group members are dedicated to the photo documentary medium and have a strong desire to record the challenging and changing events they encounter. They work on a voluntary level and at their own expense.

Several MAP Group photographers had been photographing the Australian drought since the late 1990s, but by 2006 it was readily apparent that this was no isolated event – something more formidable was emerging. A core group of photographers, most of whom had been involved with the previous rural photographic projects, met, and it was decided to try to record the climatic, cultural and social significance of this period for posterity. With the creative aid of photographer David Marks, the name 'Beyond Reasonable Drought' was settled upon and the word went out to interested photographers that a new major project was under way.

Participating photographers commenced a series of road trips, essentially voyages of discovery that would take them far and wide across our nation, as they endeavoured to understand and record what lay before them. Although we cannot claim to have covered every region and township within, I believe that we came away with good examples of the trials, tribulations and occasional joys of Australians battling the unfamiliar.

While drought, flood and pestilence are as old as the dawn of time and it appears that the earth has suffered bouts of global warming and cooling over the millennia, it is only in recent times that human intervention has weaved its way across the globe with such devastating impact.

The environment, once a fringe player on political agendas, is now a dominant issue and while the world's economic challenges demand immediate attention, the environment will ultimately muscle its way to the forefront again. Water has become the new oil, elemental for human habitation, but also essential to agricultural and industrial processes. Its power cannot be ignored.

Here in Australia, we have uprooted established ideas about the sort of country in which we live. Dryness now inhabits our national psyche, and there is a fear that things may worsen before they stabilise, let alone improve.

Yet, within that fear lie people with a great understanding of what is happening around them. Not just scientists and academics, but Indigenous people, farmers and local environmentalists, people whose historical and day-to-day experiences cannot be discounted or ignored.

What MAP Group endeavours to show you in *Beyond Reasonable Drought* is a fair indication of the problems facing us all, particularly those Australians who live inland, away from our coastlines. This book is designed to be educative and thought provoking, a vehicle to understand the changes we will face in the future. Everyone will respond to the following images in different and unique ways. We hope that these photographs will enrich your lives and bring a deeper understanding of the challenges that lie ahead.

My grandfather used to tell me, 'There is no problem that man has created, that man cannot solve'. I'd like to hope that he is right. Evolutionary progress thrives in adversity, and what the world needs now are leaders from all walks of life to come to the fore, to give us the faith, courage and vision to go forward for the sake of all humankind.

Andrew Chapman
President
Many Australian Photographers Group

< Galahs flying over farmland. Burra, South Australia, 2007, photographer Andrew Chapman

A Moment of Awakening Martin Flanagan

In the 1990s, while on a job in Horsham in western Victoria, I met a local journalist who told me water storages in the Wimmera were down, in percentage terms, to single digit figures. The number I recall hearing was six per cent. Disinclined to believe such a drastically low figure, I checked it out with the local mayor and she confirmed the fact. I was astonished. An area one-sixth the size of the state of Victoria – an area once renowned as one of the nation's 'food baskets' – was approaching the condition of desert.

Cities are large clumps of people mostly engaged in talking to one another and to people in other cities. When I came back to Melbourne, I conducted a straw poll with virtually everyone I met. The question was simple – what do you reckon, in percentage terms, water storage levels are in the Wimmera? No-one got close. No-one knew any more than I had about what was actually going on in the land around us. Something was deeply wrong and hardly anyone knew. Truth is, hardly anyone cared.

During the summer of 2006–07 – when the bushfire season in Victoria started, not, as was usual, in February, but in October – I went to a small town in the Wimmera and saw sixty hectares of wheat that looked like withered brown paper. The earth to which it clung was cracked and broken. The farmer showing me the land was in his forties. He'd bought the paddock because he remembered a time when the sandy hollow running down one side of the paddock was a river. Now it was the memory of a river, just as there were kids in the district who couldn't believe their parents' stories of floods, having never seen one.

I felt the ghost of writer Henry Lawson that day. Lawson felt the burden of despair that settled upon his father trying to work this land in the 1890s. Lawson accused his great poetic counterpart Banjo Paterson of romanticising the bush. There are photos in this book of Dagworth Station in Queensland where Paterson wrote the words for 'Waltzing Matilda' after hearing a young woman play a soulful Scottish tune upon her zither that she'd heard at the Warrnambool races.

There's even a photo in this book of the famous billabong that the swagman drowned in, only he wouldn't drown in it now. The mud on the bottom of the billabong is cracked and broken; such water as it holds is a muddy puddle. It's another sort of ghost we hear passing by this billabong now, the ghost of an Australian environment that is changing radically as the world turns around us like a giant in its sleep.

Are the global financial crisis and the global environmental crisis related? I believe so. Both come back to excessive greed which, at its most fundamental, is an imbalance. We now have to find a new balance within diminished – perhaps much diminished – means. There is a political dimension to this. There are also issues of science which can mean wading through a sea of expert opinions. This can be exhausting and ultimately misleading.

A moment of awakening came for me about ten years ago, when I drove from Burnie to Rosebery on the west coast of Tasmania where I lived as a kid. It was a journey I had made many times, but what I had seen before were the random entanglements of native forest. I won't say I loved it in a romantic sense, but I knew it was part of that place in some ancient, intimate way. Ten years ago when I made that trip again what I saw was row after row after row of tree plantations. It is trite to speak of a sense of loss arising from such an experience, but I have no other way of expressing it, and I only have to think about driving down that road again to be reminded of it anew.

An Aboriginal man I have a brother relationship with is from the Murray River. His spirit totem is the Murray cod. Some people say the Murray is dying. If it is, part of him is dying too. If I say the Murray is dying, someone will raise a hand and say, 'No, it's not,' and we will enter a long and possibly endless diversion while we argue over a definition. Let us just say of the Murray River that it is a frighteningly diminished version of itself. Let us remember that it ran through this country sustaining an abundance of life for thousands of years, and in only one hundred years we have conspired to exhaust its prodigious bounty.

I am glad that this book has grins in it. There is still a spirit in the land which is invigorating – amazingly so. Nonetheless, in travelling Australia over the past decade, I have crossed too many dried-up riverbeds not to believe some serious change is afoot in the natural world, the consequences of which could be dire.

Martin Flanagan

> This area received higher than average rainfall over two years prior to 2001 and farmers were optimistic, but the pattern reversed in 2002 when it received only fifty-seven millimetres of rain. Farmers struggled to maintain vegetation to protect their topsoil but, as in the case of this paddock, many lost all their topsoil to the wind. Near Bourke, New South Wales, 2003, photographer Peter Eve

Waiting for the Blessed Smell of Rain Timothy Lee

For anyone familiar with drought there is no smell as evocative as the promise of rain. The scent of moisture in the heavy atmosphere carries the promise of rebirth and renewal to the land and its inhabitants. Then, as the first fat droplets fall upon hot, parched ground, there is no sweeter smell in creation. It feels as though nature has at last taken a vital breath.

During the past decade, erratic seasons across much of Australia have ensured that the sweet smell of rain has been rare. The occasional dark rain cloud taunts us before dissipating into another cloudless sky. Drought comes stealthily. We measure its impact by starving stock, heat waves, shrinking dams, bare ground, cracked earth and a monotonous procession of clear skies. In the shimmering heat haze of the midday sun drought wraps its tentacles around the land and slowly saps the life from it.

Yet there is also beauty in drought. The severe drought of the 1890s, with its continual red outback sunsets, prompted poet Henry Lawson, in his work 'Andy's Gone With Cattle', to call the phenomenon the 'red marauder'. Such imagery has helped imprint drought upon our national consciousness. A summer dust storm, rolling across the horizon, seeming to devour all in its path, is an awesome sight. Dorothea Mackellar's 'wide brown land', 'her terror and her beauty' indeed.

Some country people, accustomed to years of drought, believe these severe 'dry spells' are simply nature's way of resting the ground. Many ecologists agree. They point to our specially evolved native fauna and flora and marvel at its adaptability. Australian farmers are also adapting, becoming more in tune with the rhythms and cycles of this ancient land. They are replanting native vegetation on farms where, until a few decades ago, they were given government incentives to clear it. In an effort to make farming more sustainable, scientists are evaluating the agricultural potential of native plants and animals.

Many of my most vivid childhood memories involve drought: trickling out emergency fodder onto the parched ground, the emaciated, frenzied merinos competing for the precious grain, and the crows, those black-plumed opportunists, eyeing off the dead and dying stock. At home, we sometimes had scores of newborn lambs, orphans of drought, being hand-reared on powdered milk. It was merely another chore of the many brought by drought. I have never forgotten that blessed smell when, finally, the rain came and darkened the bare earth.

Drought continues to hasten the demise of rural communities, most markedly in marginal farming regions. Where once a small community could boast several football teams, now it can struggle to field even a tennis side. Global commodity prices and dwindling margins have forced farmers to farm more land in order to survive. Bigger holdings mean far bigger machinery requirements and more corporate involvement at the expense of family farms. The population drift is marked by derelict houses and dusty, moribund towns. Urban dwellers are also seeing the impact of the drought. The crisis in the Murray–Darling Basin continues to make headlines, and years of below-average rainfall and growing populations have brought water restrictions to most capital cities and regional towns. Australia is the world's driest inhabited continent. If the predictions of climate change prove to be correct, the area of Australia's settled regions will shrink rapidly and markedly.

Beyond Reasonable Drought could not be more timely. Not surprisingly, it draws its inspiration from the Farm Security Administration photographs of the American Midwest, which, in the 1930s, conveyed to the wider world the American Dust Bowl: compelling and compassionate documentary images of crippling drought and economic collapse. Likewise, the photographs in this book say much about our national character, of resilience and laconic humour in the face of hardship. The fetid mud of an empty waterhole has become a deathtrap, and the farmer, poised above, is about to shoot his stricken stock. The bones of earlier drought victims lie bleaching in the weather. The dust clouds ascend from spidery stock trails as sheep trudge to water. Exposed riverbeds and lakes show boats beached like whales. There is human drama in the protest placards carrying angry messages for politicians about who has the right to precious water supplies.

In time, this collection will be regarded as a national treasure, and this book a family heirloom.

Timothy Lee
Senior Reporter
Landline ABC Television

> A view of the Grampians from a hill near St Arnaud, Victoria, 2005 photographer Michael Silver

Following page: In 1956, Lake Wendouree in Ballarat was nearly rejected as a site for yachting and rowing events for the Melbourne Olympics because it lacked sufficient depth over the whole course. Forty-eight years later, the Lake Wendouree Rowing Club's coxed four team long for any water at all as they stand two metres below the usual water line. Ballarat, Victoria, 2007, photographer Ian Kenins

Drought or Climate Change? David Jones

Australia is a place of climate contrasts, a land of 'drought and flooding rains'. This cycle of droughts and floods is as familiar to modern-day Australians as it was to Dorothea Mackellar when she penned the words of her famous poem over one hundred years ago.

Research by climate scientists means that we are now able to quantify scientifically that Australia is indeed a country of extremes with one of the most variable rainfall climates on earth. We also know that many of our droughts and floods are linked to climate variations in the Pacific and Indian Oceans, and particularly the variations of the El Niño–Southern Oscillation, which gives rise to the usually wet La Niña and the usually dry El Niño.

Over the last century, Australia has experienced many severe droughts. The 'long dry' or 'millennium drought' currently affects large parts of Australia. The 'long dry' is actually a series of different droughts that start at different times and cover the south-west and south-east of mainland Australia, extending up through inland New South Wales into southern Queensland.

In the south-west, the drought is a continuation of a drying trend established in the 1970s. The climate of that region is now ten to twenty per cent drier than it once was, as is the climate in the south-east, where the decline in rainfall began in the 1990s. Further north, the drought started with the 2002 El Niño event. Some modest relief in the last year was brought by the 2007–08 La Niña.

Because the 'long dry' affects the capital cities of Perth, Adelaide, Hobart, Canberra and Melbourne, many Australians are affected by drought. The story is a little different in each city, but the impacts are often the same.

Melbourne, in south-eastern Australia, is the epicentre of the drought. Since 1996, each successive year has brought the city below-average rainfall; that's twelve years in a row that have failed to receive the average of 650 millimetres, or twenty per cent below the long-term average. The run-off into Melbourne's dams has been some forty per cent below average, while some regional areas have fared even worse. The start of 2009 has been the driest on record, culminating in Black Saturday on 7 February, when temperatures reached a record 46.4°C in the city centre and 48.8°C in country Victoria. Firestorms, which blazed for several days, wiped whole towns off the map.

Why has it been so dry? The Bureau of Meteorology and the CSIRO, in collaboration with researchers across government and industry bodies, have been working to understand the current drought. The south-eastern drought started in late 1996. The subsequent El Niño years of 1997, 2002 and 2006 were each particularly dry. Ordinarily, these years would have been interspersed with wetter years, but since 1996 the intervening periods have only received average rainfall at best. South-eastern Australia as a whole has now missed out on one to two years' worth of its 'normal' rainfall since the drought began.

A notable feature of the drought in southern Australia is the substantial decline in autumn rainfall. Autumn rainfall 'wets up' the soil in catchments, allowing winter rain to flow into rivers. Autumn rain also gives crops and pastures a start after the heat and dry of summer.

The autumn drying was first noticed in south-western Australia in the 1970s; it has subsequently spread to the south-eastern states. This rainfall decline is driven by a rise in atmospheric pressures, and a weakening of cold fronts and low-pressure systems that once reliably brought rainfall to southern Australia. Scientists have linked this shift in weather systems and rainfall to human-caused climate change, caused by an increase in greenhouse gases and changes in the ozone layer over Antarctica. In recent years we have also seen a repeated failure of spring rains, which is a projected response to global warming across southern Australia.

Rising temperatures are the clearest sign of climate change. Australia has experienced substantial warming over recent decades, and the country as a whole has warmed by approximately 1°C in the last fifty years. Recent years have been up to 2°C warmer than those in the first half of the twentieth century, a difference the equivalent of moving about 400 kilometres closer to the equator. A recent CSIRO study, using observations from the Murray–Darling Basin, has shown that stream flows decline by fifteen per cent for each 1°C of warming. With a further warming of 1°C to 2°C projected by 2050, and further declines in winter and spring rainfall across the south in particular, the long-term outlook for drought is not good.

Should Australians view the current drought as the start of climate change? The current drought, clearly the hottest on record, now extends far beyond our historical experience. It is difficult to make a case that this is simply a natural cycle and that a return to more normal rainfall is inevitable. Climate change caused by humans is now acting to make droughts hotter, more severe and increasingly frequent, particularly in southern and eastern Australia. At best, the current drought might be an early warning for a hotter and drier future; at worst, it may be the beginning of irreversible climate change.

Dr David Jones
Head of Climate Analysis
Bureau of Meteorology

resilience

Like many whose farms are not producing enough to live on, Peter Jones is doing casual work on other properties to survive. Springvale North Poll Merinos, Burra, South Australia, 2006, photographer Peter Eve

> Five-year-old Steffany Cashin plays in Laanecoorie Reservoir near Bendigo. The reservoir had almost dried up, but a few days before the photograph was taken, rain covered the surface with water, increasing the reservoir's volume by three per cent. Near Bendigo, Victoria, 2007, photographer Rodney Dekker

Thunderstorms bring hope, but little rain, to this paddock in New South Wales' southwest. Waugorah Road, near Balranald, New South Wales, 2008, photographer Andrew Chapman

Sunset over the remains of a failed wheat crop, harvested for hay. The view is from the abandoned house of Bill Allen whose ancestors came to farm in the area in the 1800s. Bill bought this farm as a soldier settlement in 1947. In 1977 he moved into town but continued to farm the land until the early 1990s. Bill's son, Stuart Allen, who lives and farms in another district, now owns and share farms the land. Near Wycheproof, Victoria, 2008, photographer Jaime Murcia

A monsoonal rainstorm about to hit. Just after this photograph was taken, the storm dumped fifty millimetres of rain in a few minutes. The fields filled with water and photographer Michael Silver, unable to open the car door because of strong winds, drove slowly along the disintegrating road. When he reached the closest town, only five kilometres away, there was no evidence of the storm. Near Carrathool, New South Wales, 2008, photographer Michael Silver

Monsoonal rainstorm in the western Riverina region of New South Wales. Near Carrathool, New South Wales, 2008, photographer Michael Silver

Dick Bryan, who has been droving in the Jerilderie district for fifty years, with his grandson Andrew. Jerilderie–Uralla Road, New South Wales, 2008, photographer Andrew Chapman

> Farmer Brad Fischer walks on Lake Albert near the mouth of the Murray River. The dairies in the local area used to supply half of Adelaide's milk and in 2000 the Fischers won a national dairy industry business enterprise award. These days the farm only supports beef cattle, the deterioration of water quality having made dairy farming unviable. Lake Albert, South Australia, 2008, photographer Randy Larcombe

< Fifteen-year-old Rebecca Jackson holds the shell of a long-deceased turtle found on the banks of the Lower Murray River. Rising salt and falling water levels have made both short- and long-necked turtles susceptible to tube-worm infestation. Clayton, South Australia, 2008, photographer Randy Larcombe

Kyle Chesser and Galen McFarlane from Eastern Fleurieu School show two rescued turtles. In their own time students patrol the banks of the Lower Murray river at Clayton Bay and rescue turtles by removing the tube worms and returning the turtles upstream where water is fresher. Clayton Bay, South Australia, 2008, photographer Randy Larcombe

Under a red gum on Lake Tala in New South Wales. The lake has dried up for the first time since 1946. Michael Spinks' family property, Is-Y-Coed, is adjacent to the lake and has been destocked as the drought bites harder and a once stable water supply is no longer available. Lake Tala, Balranald, New South Wales, 2008, photographer Andrew Chapman

< The Foodbowl Modernisation Project is the name given to the north–south pipeline linking the Goulburn River with Melbourne's water storages, which involves an upgrade of the one hundred-year-old Goulburn–Murray irrigation system. Local legend and Goulburn Valley orchardist John Corboy, whose idea it was, has not always found it easy to convince farmers of the project's merits and it has proven a political, emotional and often divisive scheme. It did find favour with the Victorian Labor Government, who provided one billion dollars in funding for the project that commenced in May 2008. Near Shepparton, Victoria, 2007, photographer Julie Bowyer

Lorna and John Petrass (left) in the kitchen of their property, Drummoyne, in Victoria's Wimmera district, near Horsham. John Petrass (right) holds a photo from the 1974 flood that laid siege to his Byrneville family property for eight months. The photo shows John standing in the water and his son Greg getting out of the boat that they used to access their property. Wimmera district, Victoria, 2008, photographer Andrew Chapman

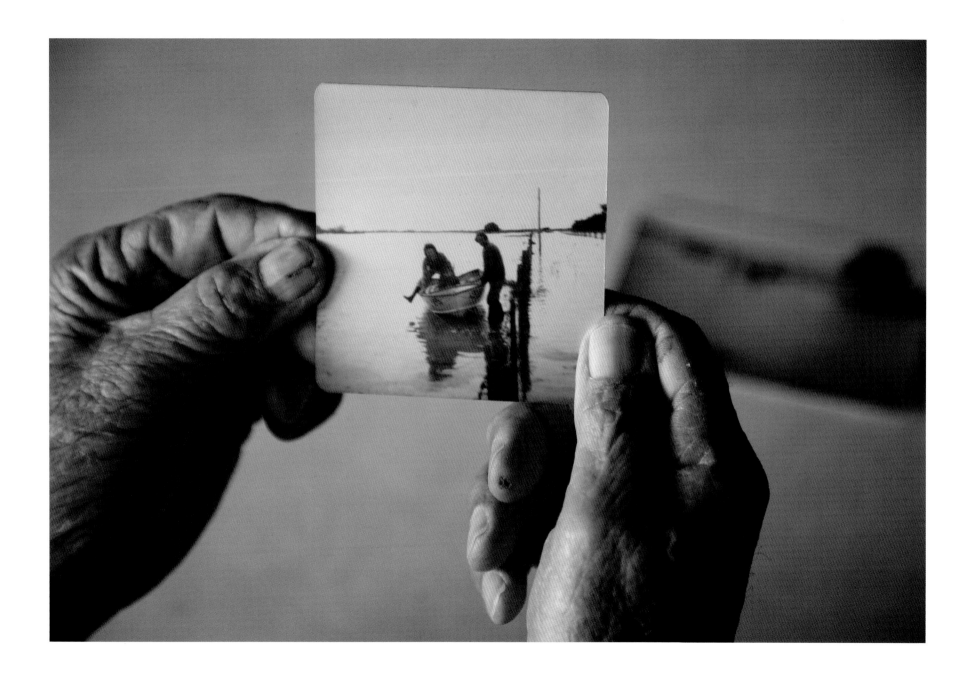

< Falling wool prices have encouraged many farmers to diversify. White Suffolk are bred for their meat and not their wool. Burra, South Australia, 2007, photographer Andrew Chapman

This photograph was taken on the last day that cattle were grazed along this stretch of the Mitchell Highway before being transported by road train to greener pastures in Queensland. With no fodder remaining and no rain since November 2000, when a total of 178 millimetres was recorded, fourth-generation grazier Laughlin Ross, with his dogs Sky and Rain, was faced with the prospect of selling his cattle and losing four generations of breeding. Nyngan district, New South Wales, 2007, photographer Rodney Dekker

A huge willy willy whips up the desert sands in Victoria's Mallee country. Between Murrayville and Ouyen, Victoria, 2007, photographer Michael Silver

> Dry river streams viewed from above resemble tree leaves. South of Rockhampton, Queensland, 2005, photographer Leo Farrell

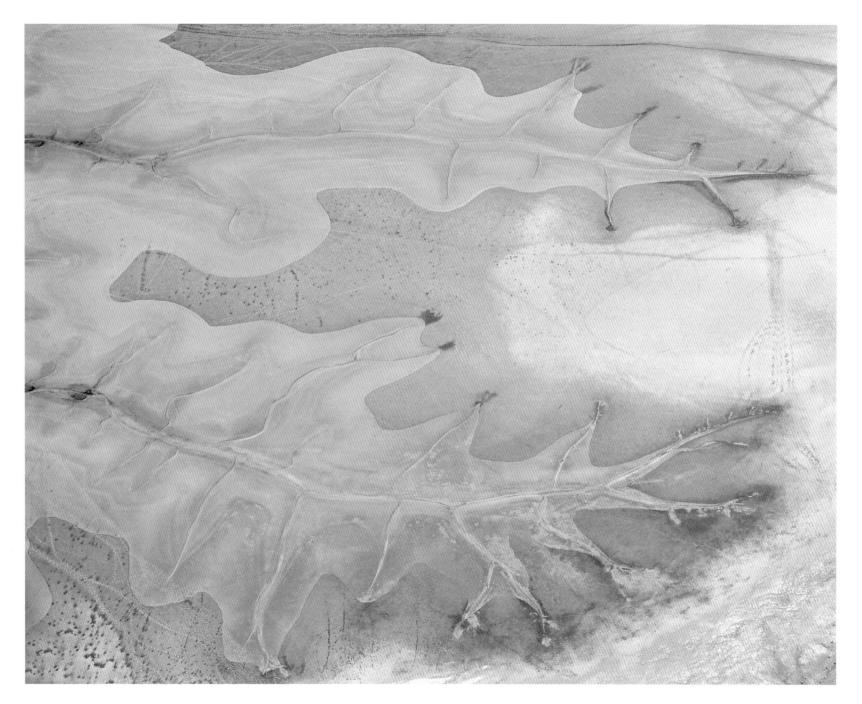

Cattle being fattened on the road between Warren in New South Wales and Roma in Queensland. Of finding water for the herd of 640, the drover remarked, 'I've just got to take it as it comes. In this game you can't plan things. You don't know what's going to happen tomorrow. I suppose that's droving, hey?' Near Warren, New South Wales, 2007, photographer Rodney Dekker

> On his Gippsland farm, beef cattle farmer Greg Grundy picks up fodder for his livestock that, due to drought and then floods, has been transported from Western Australia. Riverslea district, Victoria, 2007, photographer Rodney Dekker

A massive dust storm followed by a torrential rainstorm in wheat-growing country. The huge orange cloud of dust hit first and lasted for about ten minutes. Then the rainstorm hit and dumped fifty millimetres of water in fifteen minutes. Unable to see where he was going, photographer Michael Silver crawled along in his car at walking pace and hoped the road didn't flood – the paddocks surrounding the road were covered with water in a matter of minutes. Weja, New South Wales, 2008, photographer Michael Silver

Water buffalo walk out onto the Mary River wetlands in the predawn glow. The Top End receives an approximate annual rainfall of 1650 millimetres, most of which falls from November to the end of March. There is a huge influx of wildlife at this time of year.
Mary River wetlands, Northern Territory, 2007, photographer Peter Eve

Trying to make two ends meet ... It used to be a boating holiday village, but now Milang's jetty, on Lake Alexandrina in the Coorong, juts out over dry land with the waterline hundreds of metres away. Milang, the Coorong, South Australia, 2008, photographer Michael Silver

A common sight in drought-affected areas. Large mobs of kangaroos head for artificial waterholes on properties that source water from artesian bores. Oxley Station, Macquarie Marshes, New South Wales, 2002, photographer Michael Amendolia

Cattle farmer Andrew Jenkins plants grain to grow feed for his stock to try to take advantage of recent rain in drought-affected south-western Victoria. Carapook, Victoria, 2007, photographer Joseph Feil

> The banks of the Mary River, on the edge of Kakadu National Park, showing through the wet season cover of water. Mary River, Northern Territory, 2007, photographer Peter Eve

Rodney Grosser tends a patch of melons on his South Australian property. Rodney's grain crop failed in 2006. Sheep ate what remained and by January 2007 the landscape began to look more like a moonscape. Dutton, South Australia, 2007, photographer Andrew Chapman

> Charlie Farrar faces the wind overlooking the devastated graveyard of Mossgiel Station in south-western New South Wales. Mossgiel Station, New South Wales, 2002, photographer Andrew Chapman

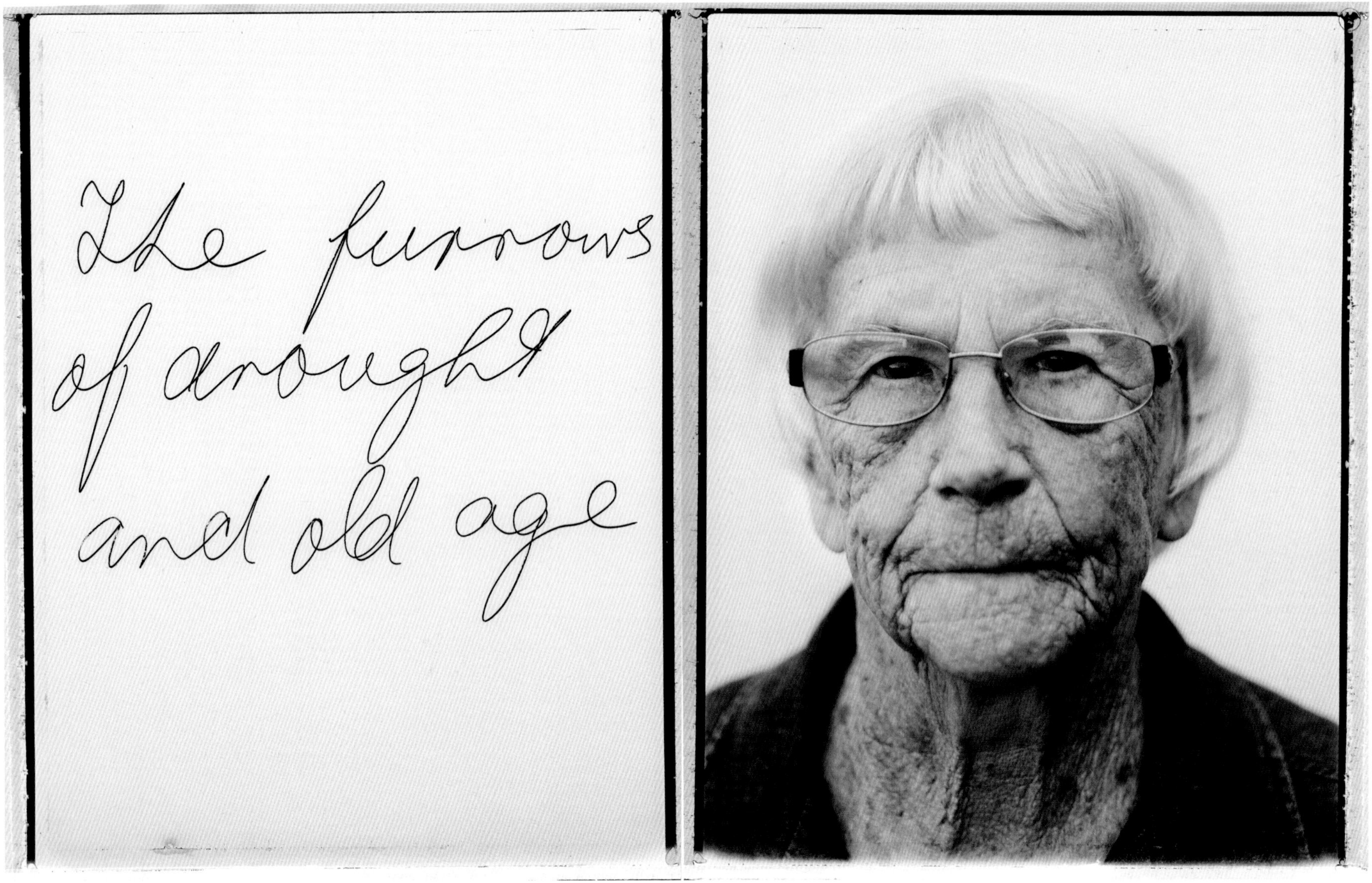

The furrows
of drought
and old age

Phyllis Davey comments on the drought.
Ariah Park, New South Wales, 2007, photographer Tobias Titz

Farmer Jim Davey comments on the drought.
Ariah Park, New South Wales, 2007, photographer Tobias Titz

Each year a
glimmer of hope
seasons will return
to normal
Maybe 2008

Geoffrey Davey comments on the drought.
Ariah Park, New South Wales, 2007, photographer Tobias Titz

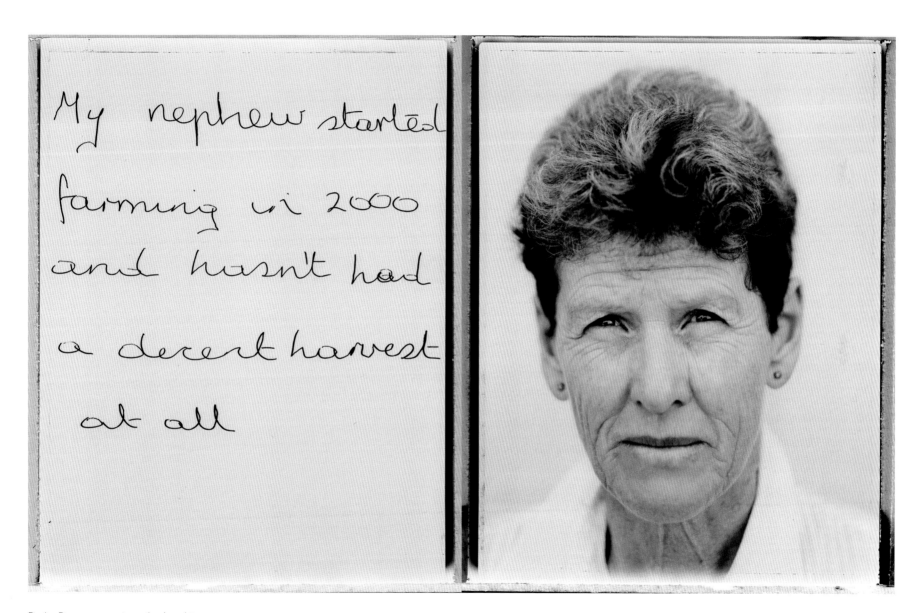

Denise Davey comments on the drought.
Ariah Park, New South Wales, 2007, photographer Tobias Titz

'Aboriginal people today understand science and climate change and this influences Aboriginal modern-day views on drought. We see the lack of rain in a spiritual way. If there was a dry spell, Aboriginal people had ways of making the rains come. But absence of rain could also mean someone has done something inappropriate to a particular site or place. We have a different connection [to country] than farmers and government mob ... we see it differently ... not just about productivity, not just a money-making venture. We should embrace country and live as one with it because that's where we come from and that's where all our spirit and dreaming is from as well. A lot of things left behind by the creator are within the country and we are told to appreciate, respect and look after it.'
Alum Cheedy, Yindjibarndi traditional owner from the Pilbara region of Western Australia, Roebourne, Western Australia, 2008, photographer Tobias Titz

Local farmhand Josh Coller takes a short break from tilling the dry land in preparation for
a potato plantation in the Hillston district of western New South Wales. Hillston district,
New South Wales, 2007, photographer Rodney Dekker

Lured far from his car by a comet-like sunset, photographer Dale Mann was thankful for electronic keys when he had to search for his black car on a vast plain on a very dark night. Hay, New South Wales, 2006, photographer Dale Mann

> A rainbow at sunset illuminates a property near Tallarook. Near Tallarook, Victoria, 2007, photographer Joseph Feil

Irrigated cotton crop near the Murrumbidgee River. The growing of irrigated cotton and rice in the Murrumbidgee Irrigation Area remains contentious amongst some locals, who claim that flood irrigation only increases salinity problems. Hay, New South Wales, 2006, photographer Andrew Chapman

> Irrigators have had their water allocations cut and some orchards will not receive any more water for the duration of the drought. This avocado orchard is one of them. In an effort to save the trees, farmers have removed all their branches. This tree's trunk has been severely lopped. The remains are painted white to reflect the heat. It is hoped that the trees will be able to survive the lack of water in this 'reduced state' and will grow normally again when the drought is over. Mildura, Victoria, 2007, photographer Julie Millowick

< Forming clouds give farmers hope, but localised rain brings them little benefit, often missing their crops and catchments. Burra, South Australia, 2007, photographer David Callow

While the Kimberley enjoys abundant water in the wet season, the dry season parches the land and graziers must move their stock to avoid over-grazing. Carlton Hill Station, the Kimberley, Western Australia, 1991, photographer Trish Ainslie

The waratas survived because they're a hardy plant, but 12 months without water the flowers aren't as strong as they should be.

'If you could only save one thing...'
Maryanne and Gary Cross,
Jamieson, Victoria, 2007,
photographer Ponch Hawkes

" I know I couldn't really save it "

'If you could only save one thing...'
Margaret Forster,
Delatite Downs, Victoria, 2007,
photographer Ponch Hawkes

A community screening of *An Inconvenient Truth*, held as part of Horsham's 'Art is ... ' Festival, in Quantong, western Victoria. Following the film, a discussion about climate change and drought was conducted by government experts and local land holders. Quantong, Victoria, 2007, photographer Krystal Seigerman

> A participant paints at a community art workshop, part of Horsham's 'Art Is ... ' Festival, Wartook. Charcoal and paints were used to interpret the previous year's bushfires in western Victoria. Wartook, Victoria, 2007, photographer Krystal Seigerman

ingenuity

< After a spell of rain, Cheong Lan collects water for her plants from her clothes line shadecloth. Orange, New South Wales, 2006, photographer Luke Wong

While parts of Australia contend with drought, others deal with flood. Australian conversation is full of anecdotes that document our struggle with such extremes. The day that yacht club worker Tim Heaney rowed down the main street to work is sure to become part of the local lore. Paynesville, Victoria, 2007, photographer Rodney Dekker

Once a common sight – but this sprinkler was quickly moved once the photograph was taken. Tugun, Gold Coast, Queensland, 2007, photographer Susan Gordon-Brown

> South-eastern Queensland was badly affected by drought, and on the heavily populated Gold Coast signs like this appeared all over the place – until the floods of 2008 dramatically changed things. Tugun, Gold Coast, Queensland, 2007, photographer Susan Gordon-Brown

A groundsman's lot is not a happy one. After over ten years of drought, many of Melbourne's suburban sports grounds are under severe pressure. Sporting injuries from playing on the hard ground are also taking their toll on players. Thornbury, Victoria, 2008, photographer Andrew Chapman

> Scorched earth near Ceduna. Near Ceduna, South Australia, 2004, photographer Leo Farrell

A house in Horsham with a very healthy-looking lawn, courtesy of fake grass. Horsham, Victoria, 2007, photographer Joseph Feil

> Fake turf on the nature strip in suburban Melbourne. Brighton, Victoria, 2007, photographer Susan Gordon-Brown

< The Foodbowl Modernisation Project seeks to save as many as 225,000 megalitres of water annually through the automation and upgrade of open channels, trunks and carriers, but there is controversy about the piping of water to Melbourne to augment the city's supply. Campaspe Shire, Victoria, 2007, photographer Julie Bowyer

By the side of a pub called the Falcon Hotel on the Murray Valley Highway, photographer Julie Bowyer found a scene that illustrates the capacity of one community to smile in the face of adversity. Kanyapella, Victoria, 2007, photographer Julie Bowyer

The almond tree in the quadrangle behind my studio
gives me pleasure all year around, but at one particular
time of year it blesses me with a gift that is both
physical and metaphysical. My birthday falls in mid-winter
in my big, cold studio, and each year the almond tree
provides me with a wonderful birthday present – it blossoms!
I am presented with both this gift of its physical
beauty and such a poetic reminder that another year has
passed and spring is soon to come!

'If you could only save one thing...'
Rod McNicol,
Fitzroy, Victoria, 2007,
photographer Ponch Hawkes

Tom comes from Yugoslavia and remembers different types
of trees. He remembers this pin oak.
He bought it as a little tree it was very small
tree, it was the right price $7.

'If you could only save one thing...'
Tom Tomic,
Mansfield, Victoria, 2007,
photographer Ponch Hawkes

I've always liked them. Mum gave
me one, I had it out front but it died.
I had it over thirty years.
    This one I bought it, it was single
stick. I paid just over $100 for this
single stick – I've had it over ten years.

'If you could only save one thing...'
Fred Dawber,
Reservoir, Victoria, 2007,
photographer Ponch Hawkes

It has a lot of age on it & I love the soft
foliage. & the Spring green colour + it goes a
beautiful apricot colour in Autumn.
Any spare water was used on this Maple.

'If you could only save one thing...'
Betty Nichols,
Mansfield, Victoria, 2007,
photographer Ponch Hawkes

Participants in Horsham's 'Art Is ... ' Festival in Wartook, western Victoria, use charcoal and pastels to interpret the previous year's bushfires. Left to right: Patricia Boyd, Kate McInnes and Jenny McInnes. Wartook, Victoria, 2007, photographer Krystal Seigerman

> Kalyanka Station's kitchen walls are decorated with paintings by the station owner's wife and a fellow artist. They remind the inhabitants of how the area looked before the drought and express an ever-present hope for rain. Photographer Juanita Wilson notes, 'It was a unique space and seemed to bind the shearers, owners and managers in an understanding that "we're all in this together".' Kalyanka Station, near Wilcannia, New South Wales, 2007, photographer Juanita Wilson

Reaching thousands of Australians affected by drought, the 'drought bus' is a Winnebago trailer converted into a fully functional mobile Centrelink office. In an attempt to alleviate the devastating impact of the drought on families, the bus's staff provide financial and psychological assistance as they move from town to town. Coleraine, Victoria, 2007, photographer Joseph Feil

> Drought bus social worker Narelle Smart takes a break outside the Heywood Post Office during her week aboard the drought bus. Heywood, Victoria, 2007, photographer Joseph Feil

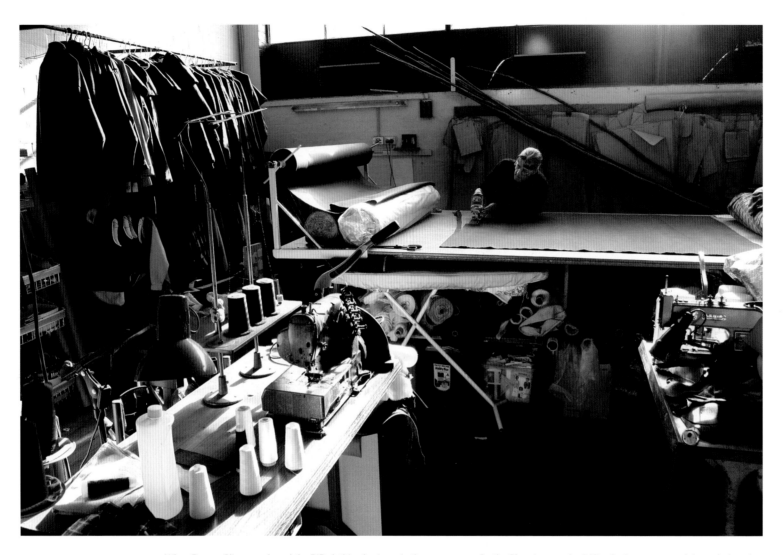

When Doreen Oliver purchased the RJR clothing business in the Geelong suburb of Newtown, there was a profitable trade in making oilskin coats for farmers. Since the drought kicked in, demand for her hand-stitched garments has fallen by fifty per cent. But when the rains came in July 2007 demand surged. 'It's so fickle,' she says.
Newtown, Victoria, 2007, photographer Ian Kenins

> On the Ghan just south of Alice Springs we passed through drought-affected country. One of the travellers observed, 'It's dusty out there'.
South of Alice Springs, Northern Territory, 2008, photographer Julie Millowick

Philip Giles in search of fresh water for his property from the ever-receding Lake Albert. His pipeline is now one kilometre from shore. Nindethana, near Meningie, South Australia, 2008, photographer Randy Larcombe

> Glen Hill, a fisher for eighteen years, heads out on the waters of the Coorong in the early morning light. The thirty-four fishers of the Coorong are committed to maintaining sustainability in their 150-year-old industry. The Coorong, South Australia, 2008, photographer Randy Larcombe

Having lived her whole life in rural New South Wales, Coleen Houston has lived through several droughts. She remembers one drought when as a teenager she had to climb up trees to cut branches for the stock to eat. As she held onto the trunk with one hand and held an axe with the other, ants crawled on her face and bit her eyelids. She says hope is so important, and having some greenery around the house keeps it alive. Budgewah, Hay, New South Wales, 2007, photographer Susan Gordon-Brown

> Ground curator Graeme Scannell sweeps the pitch at the Winter Reserve after a day's play. Scannell has been the ground's curator for twenty-five years, and says the current dry is the worst he can remember. The Geelong Cricket Association was forced to cancel matches in the 2006–07 season when Stage 4 water restrictions prevented the watering of pitches, making them unplayable. Geelong, Victoria, 2007, photographer Ian Kenins

Reed weavers Ellen Trevorrow and Noreen Kartinyeri at the Coorong's Bonny Reserve. The reeds they used to collect were up to 2.5 metres tall but they have now disappeared, forcing the local people to source them elsewhere. The Coorong, South Australia, 2008, photographer Andrew Chapman

> On Lake Alexandrina lower water levels have revealed evidence of fish trapping by local Aboriginal people, the Ngarrindjeri. A team from the University of Melbourne led by Dr Scott Heyes (here with Christine LaBond) is recording the finds. Fish were channelled into the trap and caught as the tide ebbed. Lake Alexandrina, South Australia, 2008, photographer Randy Larcombe

At Apollo Valley farm just outside Hay, 2.5 million lettuces and
1.5 million heads of broccoli, mostly destined for sale in southern
Australian shops, are produced each year. Hay, New South Wales,
2008, photographer Andrew Chapman

Mick Fischer at his property near Meningie overlooking a well that he has dug in search of fresh water for his stock. The rising salinity in the lake has forced him to sell his dairy herd and keep just 600 head of beef cattle. Behind him lies idle one of many giant pivots used for irrigation and worth as much as $100,000 each. Near Meningie, South Australia, 2008, photographer Randy Larcombe

The news on the blackboard in the Birchip pub noting rain shows scant relief from the drought for Christmas. Birchip, Victoria, 2006, photographer Rodney Dekker

> Helping hand. The Country Women's Association – always there in the background for support! Enngonia, New South Wales, 2003, photographer Peter Eve

Our 20 year old Claret Ash, we love it's summer shade
and leaves in autumn for mulch.

'If you could only save one thing...'
Nell Padbury,
Mansfield, Victoria, 2007,
photographer Ponch Hawkes

I like camellias. I think they don't
take a lot of water, there lovely flowers.
they are pretty.
They were only little babies when we brought.
them. They will be here when Fred & I are gone.

'If you could only save one thing...'
Evelyn Meehan Dawber,
Reservoir, Victoria, 2007,
photographer Ponch Hawkes

It's beautiful, it already has some age on it. You can't replace grown trees. Living away from Australia for so long gum trees represent something very special.

'If you could only save one thing...'
Ruth Lermond,
Mansfield, Victoria, 2007,
photographer Ponch Hawkes

WE HAVE LOST A LOT OF TREES INCLUDING MANY YOUNG NATIVES.

HOWEVER WE HAVE MANAGED TO KEEP ALIVE A YOUNG ORCHARD THAT THIS SEASON WILL REWARD US WITH PLENTY OF FRUITS AND BERRIES

'If you could only save one thing...'
Mervyn Ross,
Piries, Victoria, 2007,
photographer Ponch Hawkes

Stage 4 water restrictions have produced a patchwork of signs at domestic locations throughout central Victoria assuring passers-by that grey, bore or tank water only is being used on gardens. Fryerstown, Victoria, 2007, photographer Julie Millowick

> Boyd Thornbury, with watering can and tank water sign. Castlemaine, Victoria, 2007, photographer Julie Millowick

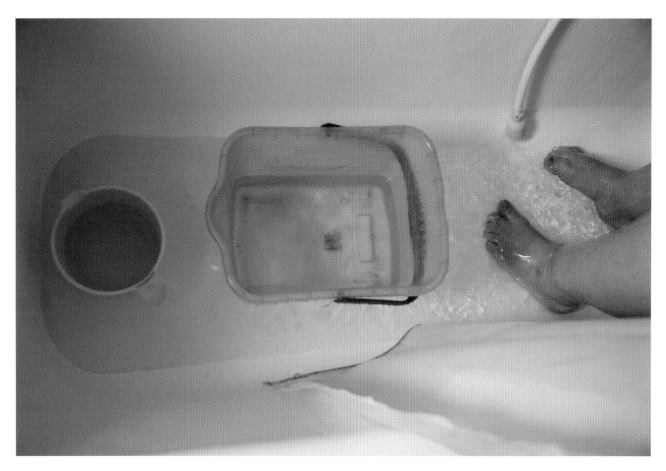

A rural woman saves water from her shower to water her garden.
Ruffy, Victoria, 2007, photographer Dale Mann

> Stage 4 water restrictions prohibit the use of water outside of the house. Residents have become inventive in finding ways to save water, such as washing clothes while they shower, and then using the resulting grey water to keep gardens alive. Two years into Stage 4, this central Victorian resident demonstrates how her shower doubles as a laundry. Fryerstown, Victoria, 2008, photographer Julie Millowick

A condition of connecting to the water pipeline being laid through
Victoria is the replacement of small farm dams with water tanks.
Combined with the wider community's leaning towards collecting and
controlling their own water supply, this has boosted demand for water
tanks. The company producing these tanks employed fifteen people in
2006. By February 2008, the company had a staff of eighty.
Marong, near Bendigo, Victoria, 2008, photographer Jaime Murcia

> Green lawns and gardens are almost a thing of the past and attract
suspicious glances from neighbours and passersby. Lawns bear the
brunt of severe water restrictions, but residents still try to keep
favourite plants alive with grey water. Broadford, Victoria, 2002,
photographer Noel Butcher

A 1600-litre tank is moved into position prior to installation in this suburban Melbourne home. Many residents have installed water tanks in an endeavour to save water. Beaumaris, Victoria, 2004, photographer Noel Butcher

The following text appears within the image on a sign:

Rainwater Carwash

Benefits/features include:
- The water recycling and reuse system will save up to 450 kilolitres of water each year.
- This catchment area has the capacity to collect up to 480 kilolitres of rainfall each year.
- Subsurface irrigation dripperlines located 150mm below the surface enables the irrigation system to come on at any time of the day or night, without disturbing the residents' use of the gardens.
- Around 2.8 kilometres of dripperline used to irrigate 1700 square metres of lawn area.
- A prototype oil change facility is also incorporated in the project. It collects waste oil from on-site oil changes to prevent contamination of the stormwater drainage system.

Rain that falls on coastal cities is a resource that goes largely untapped, and drinking water from dams is often used when untreated water could be used instead. In response to this, Melbourne Water and the Housing Commission developed a carwash that uses rainwater collected from the top storey of a nearby carpark for use by residents, such as Daniel Hay. Richmond, Victoria, 2004, photographer Noel Butcher

Sheep being fed by the manager of Tupra Station, Chris McClelland. The absence of ground covering means that stock across the drought-plagued land need food to be transported in. Oxley, New South Wales, 2002, photographer Margie McClelland

> Farmer Sandy Kidd on his property South Galway that lies at the edge of the Channel Country, a bioregion of nearly twenty-nine million hectares spanning several states. When the Channel Country floods, the nutrient-rich water turns the land green almost overnight, making it some of the best cattle-fattening country in Australia. Windorah, Queensland, 2002, photographer Michael Amendolia

< Scrub is bulldozed so that it is not out of the ground, but still attached to it with the root system intact. The tree then grows more bushy and cattle can feed from it. Enngonia, New South Wales, 2002, photographer Darren Clark

Behind Tim McKenzie, Lochmagar Station manager, is a giant blade used to slash foliage from trees that is then fed to stock to keep them alive. Near Ivanhoe, New South Wales, 2002, photographer Andrew Chapman

The lack of feed in the paddocks shows the effect of drought. Apsley, Tasmania, 2009, photographer Carol Ridgway

> This starving horse was rescued by Nancy Pattison of Spring Gully in central Victoria. The drought has impacted severely on livestock which simply cannot survive without constant hand feeding. Spring Gully, Victoria, 2008, photographer Julie Millowick

< Artist Martin King in his Brunswick studio in front of his painting *Floating is a Dream*, inspired by an artist residency in Broken Hill. Struck by the dire state of the Menindee Lakes, Martin uses motifs of birds, drought and flooding to evoke the fragility of our connections with the land and with other human beings. 'Currently the overriding factor is probably climate change or global warming so that's another impact upon a drought situation ... Everything seems more fragile and about to crack so there's a sort of sadness about it.' Brunswick, Victoria, 2008, photographer Krystal Seigerman

At Horsham's 'Art Is ... ' Festival, charcoal and pastels are used to interpret the 2006 bushfires in western Victoria. Wartook, Victoria, 2007, photographer Krystal Seigerman

Water-sensitive urban design is all the rage as town planners attempt to make use of 'free' water. Rain gardens such as these, which use water from the car park, consume the pollutants in the water, stopping them from entering the local waterways, and prevent litter from entering the drains. Footscray, Victoria, 2007, photographer Noel Butcher

> Dead European carp on the dry bed of the Hume Weir. Resident Doug Lowcock, a carp fisherman, estimates thousands of these pest fish have been trapped by diminishing water volumes as the weir has dried to 2.4 per cent capacity. Bethanga, Victoria, 2007, photographer Andrew Chapman

despair

The abandoned house (right) of Bill Allen and a view from its window. Bill's ancestors came to the area in the 1800s, and Bill bought the farm as a soldier settlement in 1947. He moved into town thirty years ago but until the early 1990s continued to farm the land around the house. Bill's son Stuart Allen, who lives and farms in another district, now owns and share farms the land. Wycheproof, Victoria, 2008, photographer Jaime Murcia

< Citrus grower Kevin Cock watches some of his trees burn. Irrigators have had their water allocations cut and they all have to decide which orchards will continue to receive water, and which will be 'let go'. Orchards that do not receive water die, are bulldozed, then burnt. Decades of hard work is lost within a matter of months. Buronga, New South Wales, 2007, photographer Julie Millowick

Communities are on heightened alert for bushfires in times of drought. The 2006 fires in the Grampians National Park burned through approximately 130,000 hectares, or forty-seven per cent of the park, exacerbating the drought's impact on native fauna. Near Willaura, Victoria, 2006, photographer Michael Silver

Photographer Julie Millowick and her son Christian McArdle. Christian spent a great part of his childhood playing at this dam in Fryerstown, central Victoria; now he can drive his ute onto it. The series of ongoing self-portraits unintentionally became a microcosm of the Australia-wide drought. Fryerstown, Victoria, 2003 (left), 2007 (right), photographer Julie Millowick

It's a much longer walk today to launch tinnies and kayaks at Milang than it was for earlier generations of shack owners. Milang, South Australia, 2007, photographer Randy Larcombe

Boat ramp and jetty at Lake Watchem that has been dry for ten years.
Watchem, Victoria, 2008, photographer Jaime Murcia

A burnt-out car at a property near Clonbinane that was destroyed by a fire
started in Kilmore, part of the Black Saturday fires of 7 February 2009, which
claimed 173 lives and destroyed over 1800 houses thoughout Victoria.
Near Clonbinane, Victoria, 2009, photographer Joseph Feil

Cattle throw long shadows in a sparse paddock as the sun rises on another hot day in the Yarra Valley. Yarra Valley, Victoria, 2007, photographer Noel Butcher

A giant dust storm rolls in over the Hay Plains. It was first thought to
be smoke along the horizon, but as it came closer, the colour became
bright orange. Hay, New South Wales, 2008, photographer
Victoria Anderson

The Yarra Glen bushfire front from School Lane, Tarrawarra, during the Black Saturday bushfires. The spot where photographer Brent Lukey stood was ablaze thirty minutes later. Tarrawarra, Victoria, 2009, photographer Brent Lukey

> Sean Doherty and Fiona Barton of Kinglake West. Sean said when they saw the fire front, 'We got out of there as quick as we could. Literally in minutes we would have been toast'. Kinglake, Victoria, 2009, photographer Australian Red Cross/Rodney Dekker

Northern Victoria, 2007, photographer Christopher Atkins

Previous pages

Pages 118-19: 'A few miles over, they've got paddocks that could fatten a crow bar.'
In the middle of a 'dry time', Donald Sampson showed photographer Peter Eve around
his property, Welbourne Hill Station on the Oodnadatta Track, where stock levels were
particularly low. Donald was still able to summon up some humour: 'Yeah, not many
trees around here. You have to have a wide-brimmed hat up here – enough shade for
you and your dog!' Near Marla, South Australia, 2006, photographer Peter Eve

Pages 120-21: Looking across barren paddocks towards the shearing shed at Ulonga
Station. One Tree, New South Wales, 2002, photographer Andrew Chapman

Lake Eildon has been the playground to generations of teenagers in the community of Mansfield. While interviewing her subjects, photographer Georgia Metaxas was told of the lost ritual of 'tagging' the Bonnie Doon Bridge. Every New Year's Eve, someone would hang off the bridge and 'tag' it – that is, until the water dropped to a level too dangerous for even the most adventurous teenager to take the risk. Left, fourteen-year-old Beth Richardson and right, seventeen-year-old Thomas Richardson. Mansfield, Victoria, 2007, photographer Georgia Metaxas

Mark Hinman and his son Thomas stand on the riverbed of the Combo waterhole, famous for being the billabong featured in Banjo Paterson's 'Waltzing Matilda'. Dagworth Station, Winton, Queensland, 2002, photographer Mark Amendolia

> Two years of below average rainfall, relentless westerly winds and overstocking have reshaped the Riverina Plain. Fences and stockyards have disappeared under windblown sand dunes, and the natural vegetation of saltbush and bluebush varieties succumb over time. More robust native bushes cling on as the shifting sand forms mounds around them. Sturt Highway to Balranald, New South Wales, 2003, photographer Margie McClelland

Optimistic that rain will fall and that a crop can be planted, farmhand Mark Sibley tills a failed wheat crop into the soil. The dryness of the land increases the amount of soil that is mixed into the air. Nevertire, New South Wales, 2007, photographer Rodney Dekker

> No water, no vegies. Boundary Bend, Victoria, 2007, photographer Jim McFarlane

Three trees, front view, Corack, Victoria, May 2007
Three trees, back view, Corack, Victoria, January 2008

Good rainfall in 2007 presented farmers of the Wimmera district
with the best sowing conditions in years. Expecting good follow-up
rain in the spring, farmers invested heavily in planting crops. But the
anticipated rain did not come, resulting in reduced yields and up to
thirty per cent of crops across the region being cut for hay.
Corack, Victoria, 2007 and 2008, photographer Jaime Murcia

> Tony Flanery on his family's sheep and wheat property, Goonawarra,
in central New South Wales. Harden district, New South Wales, 2007,
photographer Andrew Chapman

The Northern Territory's population is small and made up of many small remote communities. The backbone of transport is the humble Cessna four-to-eight seater. In the wet season, a simple two-hour flight can involve flying around small showers, like this one, or massive thunder storm cells. This one caught photographer Peter Eve's attention because it reminded him of the hand of a more powerful presence touching the pristine wetlands near Kakadu National Park.
Near Kakadu National Park, Northern Territory, 2006, photographer Peter Eve

> In 2002, sheep on Ulonga Station at One Tree were being fed grain to keep them alive. The station passed into new hands in 2007, after conditions failed to improve. One Tree, New South Wales, 2002, photographer Andrew Chapman

Judy Beazley cutting back growth on the stumps of fruit trees. The property has gone into receivership because of the drought. Bourke, New South Wales, 2007, photographer Juanita Wilson

> This image was taken at a knackery on the edge of Melbourne. After being put down, the horse is dragged by tractor into the processing area. Horses are generally obtained from sale yards around the country. Melbourne, Victoria, 2005, photographer Kristian Scott

Bushfire smoke over the You Yangs gives the sun an eerie feel. Taken from aboard the Bass Strait ferry as photographer Michael Silver sailed to Tasmania. Bass Strait, 2009, photographer Michael Silver

> Ash is all that remains after destructive fires came through Gippsland between Boolarra and Darlimurla in the days prior to the tragic fires of Black Saturday on 7 February 2009. Gippsland, Victoria, 2009, photographer Joseph Feil

< Rescuing sheep from drying dams is a daily activity for these farmers. Stuck in the mud, sheep are vulnerable to attack by predators. Crows have already started to eat this sheep alive.
Enngonia, New South Wales, 2002,
photographer Darren Clark

Shearing sheep dead as a result of drought. The fleeces are so saturated with red dust that the combs have to be changed every five sheep, instead of the usual twenty. Coonamble, New South Wales, 2002, photographer Darren Clark

High humidity sees storms deliver intense areas of rain to parched
land. Hay, New South Wales, 2008, photographer Andrew Chapman

> Michael Spinks' property, Is-Y-Coed, has been destocked as the
drought bites harder. Behind him is a dead grey box forest. Balranald,
New South Wales, 2008, photographer Andrew Chapman

Dagworth Station manager Mark Hinman is often faced with the task of euthanasing kangaroos that cannot be rescued from the thick mud of a drying dam. Winton, Queensland, 2008, photographer Michael Amendolia

> Flying across Sandy Kidd's property South Galway, which lies at the edge of the Channel Country in far western Queensland. Windorah, Queensland, 2002, photographer Michael Amendolia

By mid-February 2007, the Hume Weir had dropped to 2.4 per cent of capacity, exposing many of the original Murray River red gum trunks. Water marks indicating previous dam levels can be seen on the upper branches of this tree, towering over Bethanga resident Doug Lowcock. Bethanga, Victoria, 2007, photographer Andrew Chapman

The Stony Creek Reservoir that supplies water to the City of Greater Geelong at twenty-four per cent capacity. Geelong, Victoria, 2006, photographer Rodney Dekker

Angry farmers protest along the Goulburn Valley Highway against the
pipeline that will take water from the Goulburn Valley to Melbourne,
part of a plan to secure water supplies for Melbourne.
Near Shepparton, Victoria, 2007, photographer Susan Gordon-Brown

Around one thousand angry country Victorians march on Parliament House on
9 August 2007 to tell Premier John Brumby to 'plug the pipe' that will take water
from the Goulburn Valley to Melbourne. State Liberal/National party members also
voice their opposition. Melbourne, Victoria, 2007, photographer Rodney Dekker

The dust rises with the heat every day on Mossgiel Station in south-western New South Wales during the worst drought in memory. Hearing the truck, hungry sheep emerge from a dust storm for feeding. Mossgiel Station, New South Wales, 2002, photographer Andrew Chapman

For Tim McKenzie, manager of Lochnagar Station in western New South Wales, keeping the sheep alive is a grinding day-by-day battle. West of Ivanhoe, New South Wales, 2002, photographer Andrew Chapman

> Like a lost tribe, sheep emerge from the dust at Lochnagar Station. West of Ivanhoe, New South Wales, 2002, photographer Andrew Chapman

Mistakes are costly in times of drought. These sheep were left in a paddock without water for a day when a dust storm struck, killing over half the flock. Coonamble, New South Wales, 2002, photographer Darren Clark

Toolondo Reservoir (left) has the capacity to hold 92,430 millilitres, and Lake Lonsdale (right) has the capacity to hold 65,480 millilitres, but both were empty at the time of these photographs. These lakes come under the same water authority, Grampians Wimmera Mallee Water, which covers thirteen municipalities either fully or partially, over an area similar in size to Tasmania. When these photographs were taken in November 2006, the total volume of water held in reservoirs in the region was at 4.8 per cent. Near Horsham, Victoria, 2006, photographer Rodney Dekker

> Without protective ground vegetation, farmland is robbed of its soil by strong winds that form hazardous dust storms. Nevertire, New South Wales, 2007, photographer Rodney Dekker

Brothers David and Andrew Jenkins load grain and fertiliser into an ageing tractor, preparing to take advantage of recent rain in drought-affected south-western Victoria. Carapook, Victoria, 2007, photographer Joseph Feil

> A parched paddock near Colebrook shows the effect of four years of drought on the Tasmanian Midlands area. The drought has left the nearby Craigbourne Dam declared officially empty, and the Tasmanian branch of the Country Women's Association has run out of funds after providing over half a million dollars in drought relief since December 2006. Near Colebrook, Tasmania, 2009, photographer Dale Mann

The manager of Ripplewood Caravan Park begins cleaning up after the flood of 2007. The silt deposits are more extensive than previous flood years, a consequence of bushfires earlier in the year destroying the vegetation. Mitchell River, via Wuk Wuk, Lindenow, Victoria, 2007, photographer Rodney Dekker

> Desperate to drink, sheep become stuck in the mud, their heavy coats dragging them down. Many are rescued, but some are so exhausted they die anyway. Naringal, at Wallinduc, via Cape Clear, Victoria, 2000, photographer Susan Gordon-Brown

Richard Bowden with his dog Nuggett on his 12,400-hectare property at Bothwell in Tasmania's central highlands, which has been in his family since 1911. Richard says that in all his seventy-five years he has 'never seen it like this in Tasmania'. On this day, the shower of rain did little but settle the dust and lift the spirits of ever-hopeful farmers. Bothwell, Tasmania, 2009, photographer Melanie Faith Dove

> The area around Hamilton, in Tasmania's central highlands, has had around half the average rainfall for the past three years. Hamilton, Tasmania, 2009, photographer Melanie Faith Dove

Fifth-generation farmer Sam Dodd near the mouth of the Murray River. The water has receded 300 metres from the pre-drought shoreline and water is no longer accessible for irrigation. Of the twenty-four dairy farms in the region, only four remain operational. Lake Albert, Meningie, South Australia, 2008, photographer Rodney Dekker

> Aboriginal farm workers Neville Mark and Greg Welch stand in front of beef cattle on agistment at Raukkan Farm. As descendants of the original inhabitants of the area, Neville and Greg share a long history of belonging to the land. Raukkan Farm is one of twenty in their region to stop dairy operation. Narrung, South Australia, 2008, photographer Rodney Dekker

Usually, approximately half of the Darling River's flow is diverted for irrigation. In July 2007, the water allocation for irrigation from the Darling River was cut to zero for the first time in thirty-five years. State governments have come under fire from environmentalists and farmers for mismanagement of the river and there have been calls for the Commonwealth to take control of it from the states. Pooncarie, New South Wales, 2007, photographer David Callow

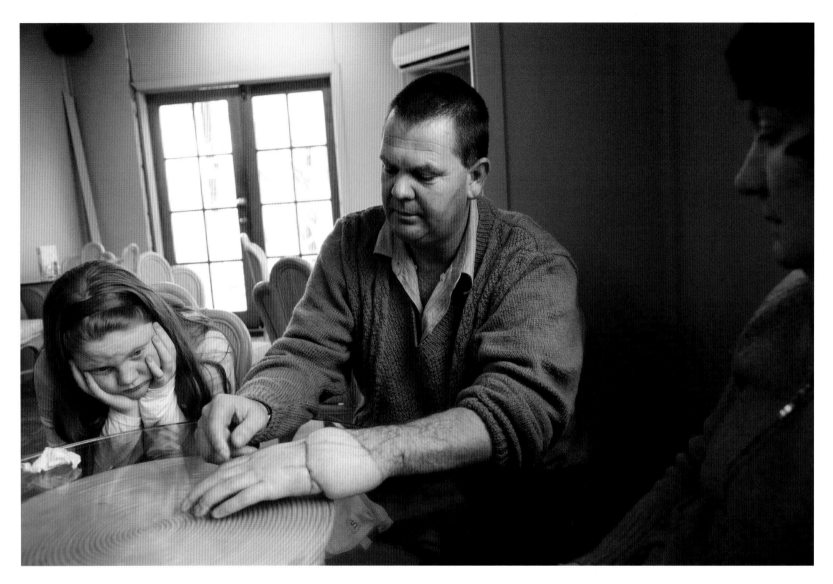

Farmer Malcolm Holm, pictured with his family, accidentally cut off his left hand in a grain machine the day after being notified that his pre-purchased water allocation was to be reduced by thirty-two per cent due to the low level of the Hume Weir. Albury, New South Wales, 2007, photographer Michael Amendolia

> Drought causes floods: Sam Horwood in the kitchen of his flood-damaged kitchen in Hawthorn, an inner suburb of Melbourne, after flash floods inundated the drainage system. The authorities were blasted by local residents for not keeping the drains clear of litter that had banked up due to a lack of regular run-off. Hawthorn, Victoria, 2004, photographer Noel Butcher

In small towns of regional Australia, the windows of long-abandoned shops reflect the diminished prosperity of the communities. *Still Empty After All These Year, (I)*. Barmedman and Temora, New South Wales, 2007, photographer Christopher Atkins

Still Empty After All These Years (II). Barmedman and Temora, New
South Wales, 2007, photographer Christopher Atkins

Despite looking green, Lake Wallace in the Wimmera's Edenhope has no water for fishing, swimming or waterskiing after drying out completely following years of drought. Edenhope, Victoria, 2007, photographer Joseph Feil

A sign showing areas for swimming and boating activities at the
Wimmera's Lake Hindmarsh, a nineteen kilometre-long lake that has
been completely empty for four years because of drought.
Lake Hindmarsh, Victoria, 2007, photographer Joseph Feil

Green Lake, which used to host fishing, swimming and waterskiing,
and was a major part of community life in Horsham, is now completely
dried out. Horsham, Victoria, 2008, photographer Joseph Feil

< A sunken boat is revealed when the water level in Lake Marma is at two per cent. Murtoa, Victoria, 2006, photographer Rodney Dekker

Chris Spence, a judge at the Horsham Fishing Competition, stands on the bed of the Wimmera River, which would normally be two metres deep. The lack of rain has meant Australia's biggest inland fishing event, which draws over one thousand competitors to the Horsham area each March, has now been cancelled for five successive years. Horsham, Victoria, 2007, photographer Ian Kenins

The after effects of the Kilmore fire that formed part of the Black Saturday fires include this burnt-out track and surrounding land, north of Wandong. Broadford–Epping Road, Victoria, 2009, photographer Joseph Feil

> A multitude of animals perished in the devastating Victorian bushfires of February 2009. This young kangaroo, lying next to the Hume Highway, is one of them. Wandong, Victoria, 2009, photographer Noel Butcher

A sign in front of a Lightning Ridge miners' camp. Potch Lane, Lightning Ridge, New South Wales, 2007, photographer Lucy Di Paolo

> Eloise and Annalise Barlow live at Carnarney Farms with their family, and their cousins live next door. David, their father, says, 'You just focus on the family. You wake up every day, kids are healthy, wife is healthy, so that is more important than any financial situation. It is tough. There are two families here ... always remember to keep supporting each other, backing each other up – that's what gets us through.' Jerilderie, New South Wales, 2008, photographer Susan Gordon-Brown

hope

< Mick and Barney Webb, from Hawker, have cattle in Merna Merna's feedlot. Burra, South Australia, 2006, photographer Peter Eve

Craig Holmes with his sons Jarrod and Alistair. Most young descendants of the ex-servicemen who were given land around Numurkah to develop for agriculture are now leaving town because of declining farming prospects. Consequently, over sixty-five per cent of the town's population is aged over fifty-five. This image is part of the photographer's *Village Series*, through which he documents the impact of modernity, migration and globalism on villages around the world. Numurkah, Victoria, 2006, photographer Michael Coyne

Farmer Howard Flanner ponders his future as a farmer. His 2006 crop, twenty kilometres north of Ouyen in north-western Victoria, was subjected to both frost and drought damage and his yield significantly reduced. Ouyen, Victoria, 2006, photographer Rodney Dekker

> Nullawil farmer Ron Pollington leans on bails of hay salvaged from his failed wheat crop. Nullawil, Victoria, 2008, photographer Jaime Murcia

< Farmer Max Burrows standing in front of a completely empty Lake Burrumbeet, twenty-five kilometres west of Ballarat. The lake is a major wetland and when holding water is a recreational area for boating, fishing and camping. Ballarat, Victoria, 2007, photographer Rodney Dekker

Ricky Dickson watering his lawn at dusk. Lachlan Street, Hay, New South Wales, 2006, photographer Andrew Chapman

The Kimberley has a huge surplus of water during 'the wet', but rapidly becomes parched during 'the dry'. At this time, drovers muster cattle gently and quietly – without shouting, whips or any aggressive coercion. This reduces stress in the cattle and produces better beef which commands a higher price. Fossil Downs Station, the Kimberley, Western Australia, c. 1990, photographer Roger Garwood

> 'I think people have to wake up and understand the difference between need and greed. I think there's been far too much greed which has been overtaking common sense in regards to managing our waterways.' George Trevorrow, Ngarringdjeri elder. The Coorong, South Australia, 2008, photographer Michael Silver

Saltpans litter the vast desolate expanse of the Mallee's Sunset Country in north-western Victoria. Some farming families have worked these same paddocks for generations. Mallee, Victoria, 2008, photographer Gary Richardson

> Many fruit growers in the Sunraysia district have put their farms on the market. Contributing factors are financial difficulties, generational transition, wine price slumps and water price increases. 'For Sale' signs have started to appear on properties that have been farmed by the same family for three generations or more. Red Cliffs, Victoria, 2008, photographer Gary Richardson

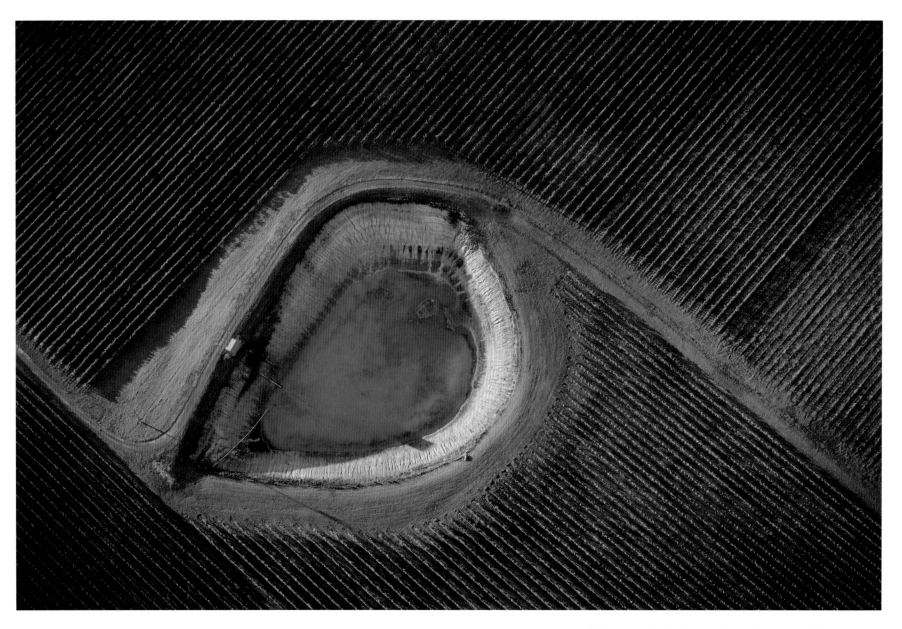

A decade into the drought, this vineyard dam east of Melbourne is typical of many in the region. Yarra Valley, Victoria, 2007, photographer Noel Butcher

It has been many years since the water level indicators at Sugarloaf
Reservoir, thirty-five kilometres north-east of Melbourne, have done
anything other than remind observers of the lack of water.
Christmas Hills, Victoria, 2007, photographer Noel Butcher

'Rural Water Commission advises boat speed of 5 knots.' Lake Eppalock, one of three catchments providing central Victoria with water, is photographed here from the Harodat Water Ski Club. Lake Eppalock, Victoria, 2008, photographer Julie Millowick

Located in South Australia's dry and dusty outback, Mount Lyndhurst is one of Australia's largest sheep stations, covering an area of 3500 square kilometres. Fully stocked, the station can run 15,000 breeding ewes and 1500 breeding cattle. Mount Lyndhurst has had no decent rain since 1991. Lyndhurst, South Australia, 2001, photographer Bruce Postle

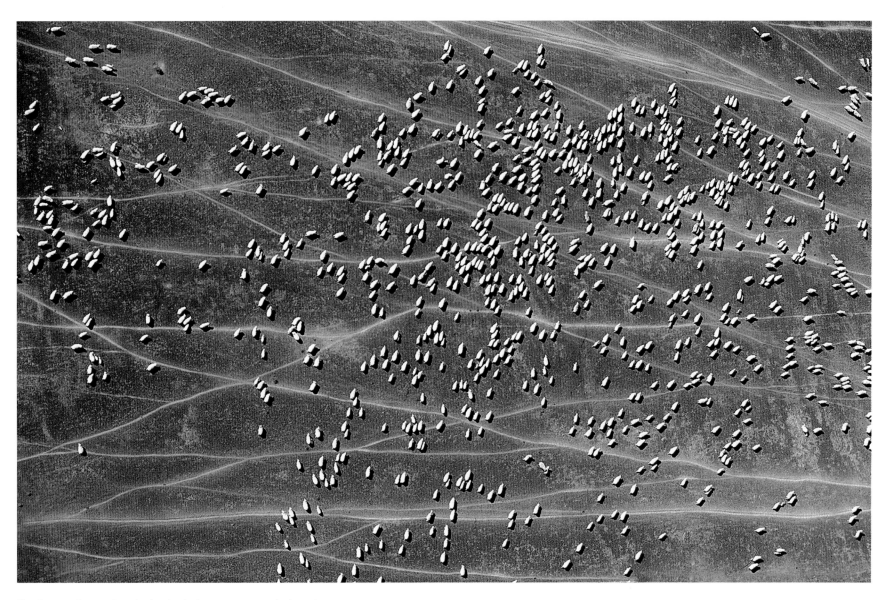

The sheep tracks worn into the dry riverbed are testament to the long absence
of rain. Lyndhurst, South Australia, 2001, photographer Bruce Postle

The Birch!!
because it is the only tree in my garden

'If you could only save on thing...'
Marta Mueck,
Mansfield, Victoria, 2007,
photographer Ponch Hawkes

I Like the old Tree if it died I will
never see anoth Tree lik this on my propaty

'If you could only save on thing...'
Werner and Gabriele Kottsiepe,
Boorolite, Victoria, 2007,
photographer Ponch Hawkes

Christian McArdle driving through the drought country of western New South Wales. Towards the end of a road trip through southern Australia to photograph the drought McArdle and his mother, photographer Julie Millowick, encountered heavy rain for two days in the lower part of the Flinders Ranges. The irony was not lost on them. Despite the rain being so heavy it cut off roads, when the rain stopped, it was as if it had never happened. South-western New South Wales, 2007, photographer Julie Millowick

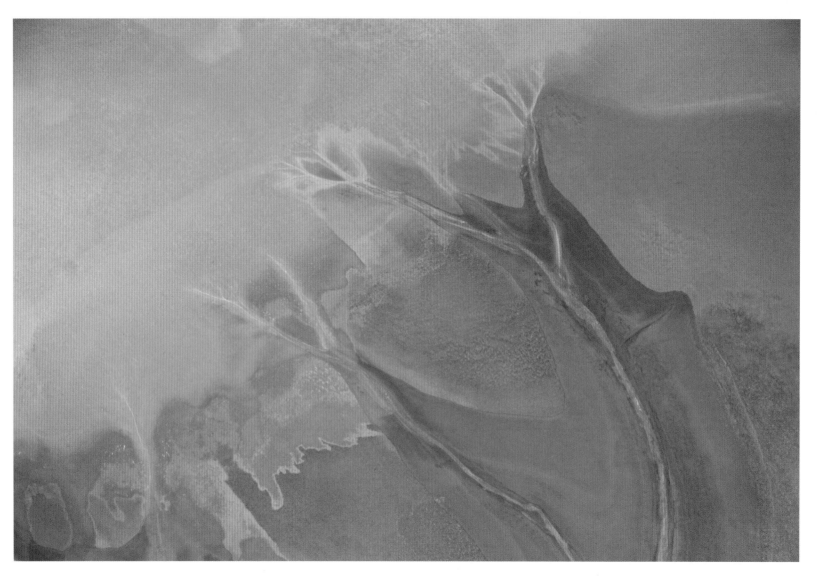

Dry river streams appear coral-like from the air, south of Rockhampton.
Rockhampton, Queensland, 2005, photographer Leo Farrell

> Pelicans over Lake Eyre in 2000. When the lake fills, the parched
earth is turned suddenly into a breeding ground for fish, birds and
other wildlife. Lake Eyre, South Australia, 2000,
photographer Bruce Postle

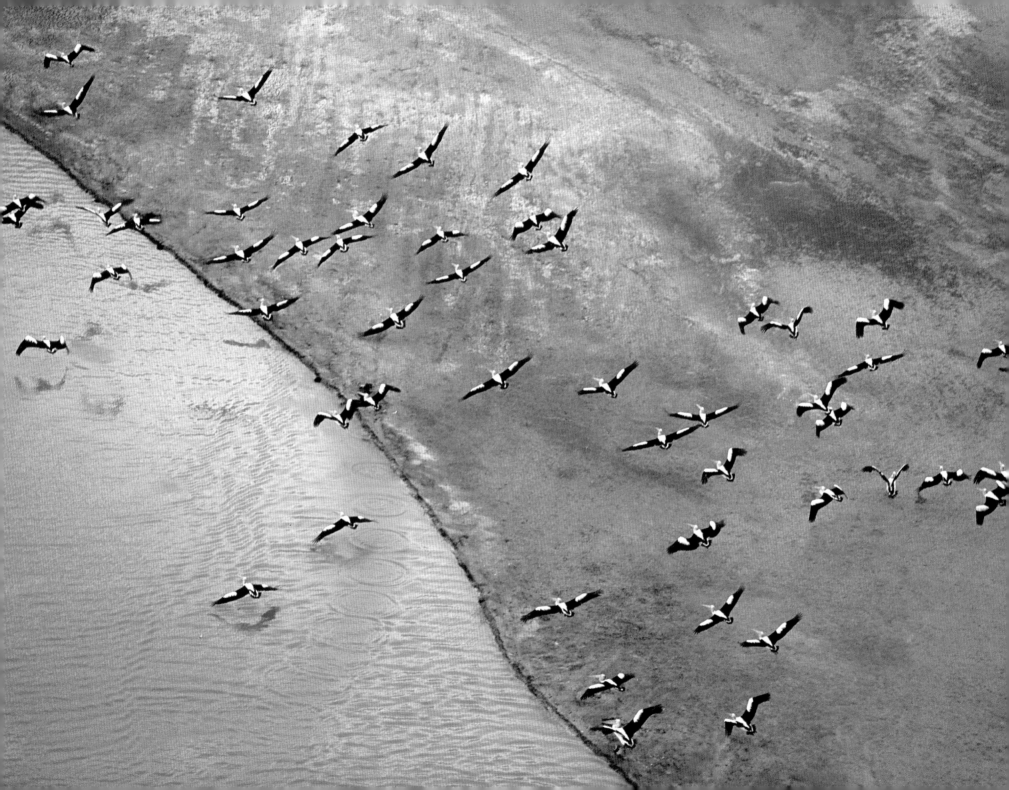

Spray watering vegetables in Gippsland.
Sale, Victoria, 2006, photographer Michael Silver

The Wimmera–Mallee Pipeline is replacing the open-channel system which, with the changing climate, is no longer sustainable. Antwerp, Victoria, 2007, photographer Nicholas Zordan

Drought reference groups have been set up across the drought-affected states to bring together farmers, scientists and other experts to advise the various governments on drought policy. Here, ecologist Dr Kerri Muller outlines to a subcommittee possible scenarios for the future of the Murray River Lower Lakes. The Coorong, South Australia, 2008, photographer Randy Larcombe

John Pargeter of Angas Vineyard chairs the Winegrape Growers Association in the Langhorne Creek region. Much of his time is now spent researching the state of the Lower Lakes and fighting for water rights. Langhorne Creek region, South Australia, 2008, photographer Randy Larcombe

Drover's wife Ros Lees watches over the campfire as dusk approaches, fifty kilometres south of Hay. Despite the solitude, heat, dust and flies, there are moments on the road that make it all worthwhile.
Cobb Highway, Booroorban, New South Wales, 2005,
photographer Andrew Chapman

> Drover Bimbo Lees watches cattle at a waterhole, fifty kilometres south of Hay. Cobb Highway, Booroorban, New South Wales, 2005, photographer Andrew Chapman

Dead trees in the Alpine National Park along Maroka Road in Victoria's high country. Alpine National Park, Victoria, 2007, photographer Michael Silver

Four months after raging bushfires fuelled by drought-bitten land
threatened the Mount Buller Village, signs of the large fires remain
as the bush re-establishes itself. Mount Buller, Victoria, 2007,
photographer Joseph Feil

Basket-maker and teacher Virginia Kaiser explores the Darling River's tenuous state through her series *River Stories*. Acknowledging local Aboriginal tradition, the vessels are made from natural materials and contain items relating to the river's destruction, such as carp bones and cotton. Broken Hill, New South Wales, 2007, photographer Krystal Seigerman

Chris Nicholls paints in his studio. Chris has always had a deep connection
to the land. 'The past is a track I travel often. Wandering inland creeks
and rivers, clambering over fallen trees with their massive root systems
exposed, providing dark resting places for secret dreaming.' Chris's current
work, entitled *My River Paintings*, depicts the degradation of rivers caused
by the drought. Wal Wal, Victoria, 2007, photographer Krystal Seigerman

Artist and lecturer at Ballarat University's Horsham campus, Ewen Ross
stands in front of his work from the series *The Green Pick*, which reflects
the slow return of growth to a region severely affected by the drought.
Horsham, Victoria, 2007, photographer Krystal Seigerman

Using the proverbial three monkeys, artist and teacher Geoff DeMain's drawings reflect the government's culpability in the continuing destruction of the Darling River. Broken Hill, New South Wales, 2007, photographer Krystal Seigerman

It's 5 am at the Ballarat Saleyards and these lambs are being drafted into size and weight categories in preparation for auction later in the day. As it becomes increasingly difficult to supply stock with food and water, farmers are forced to sell their livestock. Ballarat, Victoria, 2007, photographer Rodney Dekker

> Toby the horse makes use of any available grazing ground, in this case the next-door neighbour's yard. His owner feeds him supplementary food daily to keep him in good condition. The tiny township of Avoca in central Tasmania, sits between Fingal and Royal George valleys, two of the regions in Tasmania hardest hit by drought. Avoca, Tasmania, 2009, photographer Melanie Faith Dove

Lake Eildon in winter. Scrub is becoming more permanent and more
of the dead trees have been cleared. Lake Eildon, Victoria, 2008,
photographer Susan Gordon-Brown

> Summer rain floods a paddock near Harden in central New
South Wales. Harden district, New South Wales, 2007, photographer
Andrew Chapman

Water pumped in from the Murray River, via Chalka Creek, has recreated the wetland environment needed for regeneration of this red gum forest at Hattah-Kulkyne National Park. This has been done at the expense of farmers and, in seasons where water allocations are tight, has not been welcomed by all. Mildura, Victoria, 2006, photographer Andrew Chapman

> The Butler family on their farm in Perenjori in Western Australia's wheat belt. This tough and unforgiving country is very marginal land to farm and the family has been through some hard years. Perenjori, Western Australia, 2007, photographer Nicholas Zordan

Photograph Locations

Numbers identify page on which each image appears

Darwin

29 33 | 130

47

180

40

Northern
Territory

124 140

71

Queensland

25 194

95 141

Brisbane

54 55

Western
Australia

118

195

South
Australia

213

188 189

Perth

57

New South Wales

See inset opposite

Sydney

vii 8 22
46 174

34

Canberra
ACT

Adelaide

15 16 17 30
72 73 76 77
79 110 111 158
159 181 198 199

Victoria

Melbourne

98 156

Tasmania

209

157

153

Hobart

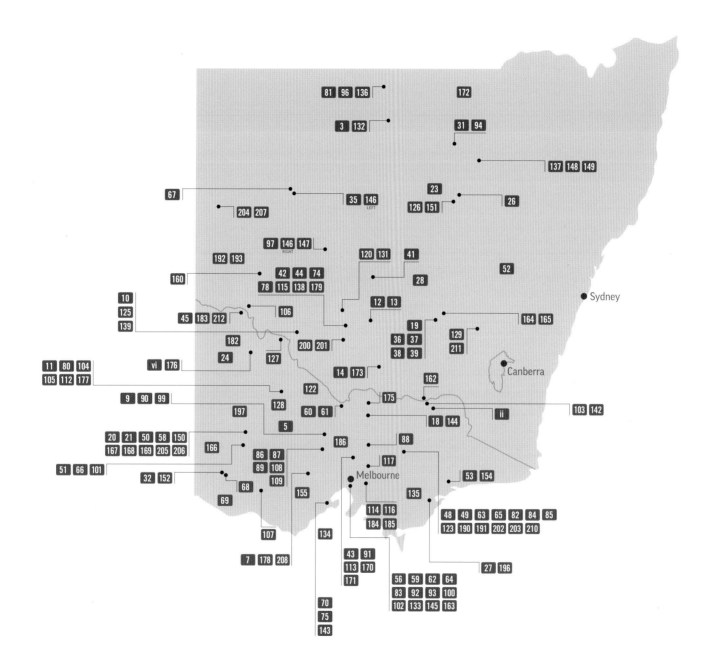

81 96 136   172

3 132   31 94

137 148 149

67   35 146
LEFT

204 207   23
126 151   26

97 146 147
RIGHT

192 193   120 131   41
52

160   42 44 74   28
78 115 138 179

10   12 13   Sydney
125   45 183 212   106
139   164 165

182   19
11 80 104   200 201   36 37   129
105 112 177   vi 176   24   127   38 39   211

9 90 99   14 173   162   Canberra

128   122   175   103 142
197   60 61
20 21 50 58 150   5   18 144   ii
167 168 169 205 206   166   86 87   186   88
51 66 101   89 108   117
32 152   109   53 154
68   155   Melbourne   135
69   114 116   48 49 63 65 82 84 85
107   184 185   123 190 191 202 203 210
134
7 178 208   43 91   27 196
113 170
171   56 59 62 64
83 92 93 100
70   102 133 145 163
75
143

Acknowledgements

The Many Australian Photographer's Group (MAP Group) is a non-profit association of approximately fifty photographers who share a passion and commitment to high quality, independent documentary image making. We are primarily involved in recording rural environments, and we donate all imagery back to the towns and people involved – a gift that enriches their historical archive in a unique and substantial way. We are also donating half of the royalties from this publication to Australian Women in Agriculture (AWiA), in recognition of the support they provide to rural communities across the country.

The travelling exhibition entitled Beyond Reasonable Drought was developed by the Museum of Australian Democracy in association with the MAP Group. The exhibition premiered at Old Parliament House in 2008 as part of Vivid – the National Photography Festival. The exhibition continues to tour under the management of The Museum of Australian Democracy. Exhibition and touring details can be found at www. moadoph.gov.au/brd. We would like to thank The Museum of Australian Democracy for its generous support of this MAP Group initiative.

We are very grateful to all subjects of the photographers, who gave their time and help most graciously.

We would like to thank the State Library of Victoria, in particular, Shelley Roberts, Madeleine Say and Margot Jones, for their support and assistance. We would like to thank The Five Mile Press, in particular Janet Rowe, Lesley Williams and Julia Taylor for their enthusiastic support. And thank you to Phil Campbell for his excellent design.

We would also like to express our thanks to the writers Martin Flanagan, Dr David Jones, Timothy Lee and Don Watson for their splendid words.

And finally thanks to Zoe Hamilton, Ben and Kate Barlow, Tim Anderson Bonsor, John Crook, Sir Samuel Moggs Foundation, Michael Field, Margo Fitzgibbon, newNorth Fine Art Printing & Gallery, Ray Stack, Stacks Financial Services and Anna Wolf.

MAP Group

Photographers

Trish Ainslie
Michael Amendolia
Victoria Anderson
Christopher Atkins
Julie Bowyer
Noel Butcher
David Callow
Andrew Chapman
Darren Clark
Michael Coyne
Rodney Dekker
Lucy Di Paolo
Melanie Faith Dove
Peter Eve
Leo Farrell
Joseph Feil
Roger Garwood
Susan Gordon-Brown
Ponch Hawkes

Ian Kenins
Randy Larcombe
Brent Lukey
Dale Mann
Margie McClelland
Jim McFarlane
Georgia Metaxas
Julie Millowick
Jaime Murcia
Bruce Postle
Kristian Scott
Krystal Seigerman
Michael Silver
Gary Richardson
Carol Ridgway
Tobias Titz
Juanita Wilson
Luke Wong
Nicholas Zordan